# Literacy Magic

## Using the Harry Potter series to inspire and extend high ability students

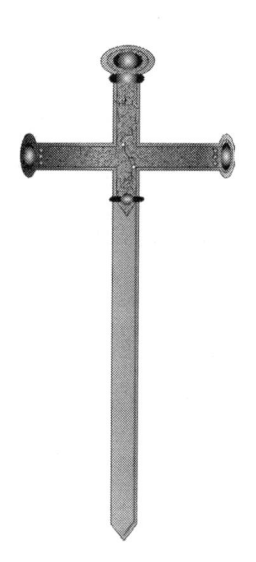

Selena Gallagher, PhD

essential
**resources**

Title: Literacy Magic
Using the Harry Potter series to inspire and extend high-ability students

Author: Selena Gallagher

Editor: Tanya Tremewan

Designer: Red Sea Books

Book code: 5579

ISBN: 978-1-927143-12-4

Published: 2012

Publisher: Essential Resources Educational Publishers Limited

| **United Kingdom:** | **Australia:** | **New Zealand:** |
|---|---|---|
| Units 8–10 Parkside | PO Box 906 | PO Box 5036 |
| Shortgate Lane | Strawberry Hills | Invercargill |
| Laughton, BN8 6DG | NSW 2012 | |
| ph: 0845 3636 147 | ph: 1800 005 068 | ph: 0800 087 376 |
| fax: 0845 3636 148 | fax: 1800 981 213 | fax: 0800 937 825 |

Websites: www.essentialresourcesuk.com
www.essentialresources.com.au
www.essentialresources.co.nz

Publisher's note: This book has not been prepared, authorised or endorsed by J.K. Rowling, the publishers or distributors of the Harry Potter books, or Warner Bros. Entertainment.

About the author: Selena Gallagher is a teacher who has worked with gifted students in Australia, the UK and China. She recently completed her PhD in gifted education and is currently setting up and managing a gifted education programme in an international school. Selena discovered Harry Potter in 2001 and became instantly hooked. She has been developing and delivering Harry-related activities to gifted learners for the past five years. She is still secretly hoping that her Hogwarts letter has been lost in the post.

# Contents

# Introduction

*Literacy Magic* is an opportunity to work some magic of your own, weaving together J.K. Rowling's spellbinding Harry Potter series with numerous challenging and imaginative activities to inspire and extend your gifted students. Imagine the impact that we can have as teachers by introducing our students to this life-changing book series, and by allowing those who have already discovered it for themselves to explore all the depth and complexity it has to offer. As J.K. Rowling herself has said, "We do not need magic to change the world, we carry all the power needed inside ourselves already: we have the power to imagine better."

This resource is designed to help you guide your gifted students to realise that power. There are activities here for everyone, whether you are looking for extension activities for an individual student in your class, activities to suit a group of students working together in the regular classroom or in a withdrawal group, or for a whole-class themed unit. It is anticipated that the activities will be most likely to suit more able students in Years 5 to 8, although this obviously depends on the level of ability of your own group of students. Some modification or additional scaffolding may be needed in some instances.

Specific suggestions about how to put the activities in this resource to use in your classroom are set out after we look in more detail at why this incredible series has so much potential to assist your gifted students in their learning.

# Why Harry?

Harry Potter is more than a fictional character. He is a cultural phenomenon. J.K. Rowling's seven-book series has sold more than 400 million copies, been translated into 67 languages and broken record after record in both the publishing and the film worlds. Starting with the fourth book, *Harry Potter and the Goblet of Fire*, each successive release smashed the record of the previous one in terms of the number of books produced in an initial print run. *Harry Potter and the Deathly Hallows* became the fastest-selling book in history, with 15 million copies sold worldwide in the first 24 hours of its release. Many have tried to explain the phenomenal success of the series, but it almost seems to defy explanation.

We can, however, point to some reasons why the series can touch, enthuse and potentially extend gifted students in particular. The following are some important features that help to explain its value in this area.

## In-depth issues

At its heart, the Harry Potter series has a great story. A surface reading reveals an entertaining story of a quest, a coming-of-age, the triumph of good over evil. But the more you think about it, the more there is to discover. A deeper reading reveals incredible intricacies and complexities (Anelli, 2008). The most obvious themes in the series include death, choices, love, power and prejudice. In academic books and journals and at fan conferences and symposiums, complex issues are highlighted and debated. Some examples of thought-provoking investigations (from Baggett & Klein, 2004) are:

☆ All the minister's men: Analysing power and the press in Harry Potter
☆ Goblins, centaurs, house-elves and werewolves, oh my!: The construction of otherness and disability in Harry Potter
☆ Is the best mum a dead mum? Parenting in the Potterverse
☆ Feminism and equal opportunity: Hermione and the women of Hogwarts.

So there is plenty of meat here for gifted readers to get their teeth into. Their advanced emotional maturity may mean that they are ready to discuss the types of issues and themes referred to above before other students of the same age. The high fantasy genre, to which Harry Potter belongs, tends to have an inherent appeal to gifted readers, who can see beyond the surface of a story to the spirit contained within (Halstead, 2009). Additionally, well-read students enjoy the sophisticated word-play, the influence of Latin on invented language and the allusions to existing mythology (Gross et al, 2003).

# Role models

J.K. Rowling herself presents an obvious role model for young gifted girls in particular, clearly demonstrating the importance of resilience. What would have happened if J.K. Rowling had been disheartened and given up when her book was initially rejected by publishers?

In her characters, students – especially gifted ones – can also find role models with whom they can identify. Hermione is the obvious choice, appearing as the typical image of a gifted child, always top of the class, reading text books for fun and answering every question in class. Witness the sometimes negative reactions this behaviour engenders from her classmates, and even sometimes, from teachers.

**"Five more points from Gryffindor for being an insufferable know-it-all."**

Professor Snape to Hermione,
*Harry Potter and the Prisoner of Azkaban*, Chapter 9

In contrast, Harry is a talented Quidditch player and this sporting giftedness is welcomed and celebrated by his fellow students. Although he sometimes struggles with his studies, he demonstrates a natural affinity with Defence Against the Dark Arts and is adept at problem solving. He also demonstrates strong leadership qualities, a trait that is often associated with gifted students. Other common gifted characteristics seen in Harry include his advanced moral development and his concern with justice and fairness.

Ron represents the invisible or underachieving gifted student. We are given early evidence of his intellectual ability through his brilliant chess-playing skills, but he is not motivated to study like Hermione is and often feels overshadowed by his older brothers. However, it is Ron, not Harry, who is selected as prefect in his fifth year, so presumably Dumbledore at least spotted his potential. He also displays intense loyalty worthy of a Hufflepuff!

Outside of the books but within the Harry Potter phenomenon, other potential role models emerge. In 1999 as a 12-year-old homeschooler Emerson Spartz created his own Harry Potter fansite. Mugglenet. com is now the most popular Harry Potter website on the internet, was visited by more than 25 million people in 2010 and generates over US$1 million of revenue each year. By the time he was 17, Emerson had been personally invited by J.K. Rowling to visit Edinburgh and interview her on the day of the release of the sixth book in the series. (For more on websites that can act as additional resources, see the References section at the end of this book.)

# Beyond the books

One of the enduring legacies of the Harry Potter series has been the creativity it has inspired in its fans, a consequence of particular relevance and value to gifted students.

The World Wide Web is awash with examples of ingenuity impelled by the Harry Potter series. The popular website fanfiction.net alone contains more than half a million "fanfics" set in the world of Harry Potter – creative writing inspired by the series. With the internet today's young readers can engage more actively with their reading material than ever before. Crafting a fanfic allows students to recognise and utilise archetypes and motifs in their own and others' literature (Mathew & Adams, 2009) and to extend or elaborate on the author's original work. When they post it online (with appropriate safeguards), they gain a genuine audience for the work and possibly useful feedback from their readers as well.

Readers' interpretation of the work of J.K. Rowling is not limited to the written word. Other responses include fanart, a series of Harry Potter puppet plays, a full-length Harry Potter musical (and sequel!) and, from one very patient fan, a stop-motion animation of *Deathly Hallows – The Movie*, using Lego. The series has also inspired the creation of a new musical genre – Wizard Rock or Wrock. Bands with names such as Harry and the Potters, Draco and the Malfoys, and Ministry of Magic sing about events in the books, the power of love and their assertion that "Voldemort can't stop the rock"!

From Wizard Rock came wizard activism. The Harry Potter Alliance is a charitable organisation that fights the Dark Arts in the real world using the power of Harry Potter. With a catch cry of "the weapon we have is love", the HP Alliance uses parallels in the Harry Potter books to educate and mobilise young people around the world in relation to issues of literacy, equality and human rights. J.K. Rowling has long been credited with turning kids on to reading, encouraging a generation of digital natives to rediscover the joy of a good book, but for James Thomas, an English professor in the United States, it goes much deeper than that:

> They've made millions of kids smarter, more sensitive, certainly more literate and probably more ethical and aware of hypocrisy and lust for power. They've made children better adults, I think. I don't know of any books that have worked that kind of magic on so many millions of readers in so short a time in the history of publications.
>
> James Thomas,,quoted in Gibbs (2007)

For gifted students, noted for their originality and resourcefulness, the possibilities that this series opens for their creative activities are virtually limitless.

# How to use the activities in this resource

By their very nature, these *Literacy Magic* activities have a strong literacy basis. They are, after all, inspired by a hefty seven-book series which naturally assumes that students will be highly competent readers. As well as extending able students in literacy, most activities address at least one other area of learning such as critical thinking, problem solving or argument and reasoning. The activities also allow you some versatility in the way that you use them, as they can be used in different ways to suit students' needs and are suited to a variety of grouping arrangements.

The table on page 7 provides an at-a-glance guide to which areas are addressed by each activity, as well as the grouping arrangements most suitable for it. Some suggestions for the broader context in which you set the activities follow.

## Bringing Hogwarts to life

One of my favourite ways to use these activities is to devote about two days to extension work (which the kids will love, because they get to miss out on "normal" school!). This arrangement gives you the opportunity to totally immerse the students in the Hogwarts experience.

You can begin by setting the scene with some Harry-inspired decorations. Film or book posters are good, and you might be able to persuade your local cinema or bookshop to give you some. Dressing up also helps set the mood. You can insist that students call you "professor" for the duration of the dedicated extension time too.

Everyone knows that new students at Hogwarts need to be Sorted into a house by the Sorting Hat, so this is the first thing you should do at the start of the extension time. Unless you have a talking hat handy, you will need to use an ordinary witch's hat (such as one of those sold around Halloween). Write the four Hogwarts house names (Gryffindor, Hufflepuff, Ravenclaw and Slytherin) on separate slips of paper and put them in the hat. Students pick one slip of paper each out of the hat in order to be Sorted into their houses. Being Sorted by the hat in this way usually eliminates any complaints that you might ordinarily get if students are not put into groups with their friends. You might also make small laminated house ID badges which students can wear to declare their allegiances.

Students then stay in their houses for group work for the duration of the extension time. Many of the activities have an element of competition and a sense of house unity will soon develop among the students.

House points can be awarded throughout the extension time. You might give each group a house point jar, into which their house points go as they collect them. I have successfully used jellybeans to represent house points. Someone will always ask if they are allowed to eat them as they earn them, and I always tell them that they can eat them if they choose, but that will mean the jelly beans won't be there to be counted at the end of the extension time when the House Championship will be decided. The competitive edge kicks in and the house points are always left untouched! It's a great lesson in delayed gratification. At the end of the extension time the points (jellybeans) are counted and the House Champions announced. Then all groups get to share their edible house points among their members.

If you are using the activities during this dedicated extension time, you might like to rename them where appropriate to fit the subjects taught at Hogwarts. So, for example, the anagram activity becomes Transfiguration, the levitation challenge becomes Charms, and Hagrid's breeding experiment becomes Care of Magical Creatures.

Activity overview

| ACTIVITY | FOCUS AREA(S) | GROUPING ARRANGEMENT(S) |
| --- | --- | --- |
| Investigating potions | Science, problem solving | Small groups |
| The hero's journey | Literacy (writing), critical thinking | Individual, pairs, small groups |
| Anagrams never lie | Literacy (reading), problem solving | Individual, pairs, small groups |
| What's in a name? | Literacy (reading), creative thinking | Individual, pairs, small groups |
| How well can you spell? | Literacy (reading), creative thinking | Individual, pairs, small groups |
| What's your Boggart? | Drama, critical thinking | Large group |
| Hagrid's experimental breeding programme | Visual art, creative thinking | Individual, pairs |
| A potty perspective | Literacy (writing) | Individual |
| Ordinary Wizarding Levels (practice questions) | Creative thinking | Small groups |
| Wingardium Leviosa (the levitation challenge) | Creative thinking, problem solving | Small groups |
| Literary lifeboat | Literacy (speaking and listening), argument and reason | Large group |
| Hogwarts staff meeting | Literacy (speaking and listening), argument and reason | Small groups, large group |
| Dynamic discussion | Literacy (speaking and listening), critical thinking | Small groups, large group |
| Learning ladders | Multiple | Individual, pairs, large group |

# Wizard withdrawals

For a group of students who are withdrawn from the regular classroom for extension in English, these activities could provide a focus for a term's work, with one or two activities completed each week. If numbers permit, students can still be grouped into houses to maintain continuity from week to week. However, using jellybeans for house points may not be such a wise choice over an extended period – buttons or beads could be used instead, or students could create a visual tally system. This kind of arrangement could also work for an after-school enrichment club.

# In the regular classroom

If you just have a few students in your class in need of extension in literacy, you can still use most, but not all, of these activities. While the rest of the class is working on the regular curriculum, a small group of more able students can work on the extension activities presented here. However, while most of the activities can be worked on by students independently, some input from the teacher, teacher aide or teaching assistant will help to get the most out of them.

Likewise, if you have only one student in your class in need of extension, there are some activities, such as the Learning Ladders, suited to individual independent work. However, if it is possible to find another like-minded student so that they can work on the activities together, it may be preferable. The process of making meaning and developing understanding can be greatly enhanced by the opportunity to share learning experiences and discuss them with peers of similar ability.

# Must students be Harry Potter fans to complete these activities?

Clearly Harry Potter fans of all ages will enjoy engaging with the books on a higher level and working on these challenging complementary activities. But what if you have some highly able students in your class who are not yet fully fledged Harry Potter fans – can you still use these activities with them?

The answer is, in some cases, yes. An in-depth knowledge of the world of Harry Potter is a prerequisite for some, but not all, of these activities. If you have students who have seen some of the films but not yet read the books, they may still be able to participate in many of these activities. Hopefully, their participation will inspire them to go on and read the books for themselves. If so, it can be useful to ask them to complete the Learning Ladder tasks specific to the book they are reading, as an independent learning project during in-class literacy times, so that they extend their understanding as they go.

---

Please note:

The website addresses (URLs) given in this book are correct at the time of publication. However, website addresses can change, and some websites may adopt advertising that is inappropriate for the classroom. It is therefore advisable to check each website you plan to use in the classroom before actually using it with your students. Essential Resources and the author take no responsibility for the content of any website included in this book.

All information provided in this book is general information that the author believes to be accurate and up-to-date at the time of publication. Neither Essential Resources nor the author will be held liable for loss or injury resulting from any action taken by reliance on information in this book.

---

# Investigating potions

## Focus areas

Science, problem solving

## Organisation

Students should work cooperatively in their house groups.

## Resources

Red cabbage
Water
Baking soda
White vinegar
Lemonade or any of the carbonated lemon soft drinks that go under a brand name
Ammonia (clear if you can get it, but cloudy will do)
4 small clear bottles
20 clear plastic cups
One copy of the **Revealing Riddle** (page 12) for each group
One copy of the pH scale (page 11) for each student
Label for each bottle of Revealing Solution – (optional) (see template label below)

> In this two-stage activity, students work with "magic potions" to explore
> the properties of bases and acids.

## Preparation

1. A day or two before carrying out the activity (no earlier), prepare the Revealing Solution. Chop up some of the red cabbage, put it in a saucepan with some water and boil it for as long as you can stand the smell – 20 to 30 minutes will do. Let it cool, then strain off the liquid and divide it among the four small bottles. You can label the bottles using the label template provided below or, if you're feeling especially creative, make labels of your own.

2. Prepare the plastic cups. You will need one set of five cups for each group, clearly labelled: A, B, C, D and E.

3. Prepare a set of potion name cards for each group. A piece of folded card works well. The potions are as follows:

   Shrinking Solution
   Ageing Potion
   Veritaserum

   Draught of Living Death
   Essence of Gillyweed

Revealing Potion: sample label

Hector Dagworth Granger's
**Revealing Solution**
Most Extraordinary Society of Potioneers
Investigating Potions

# What to do

## STAGE 1

1. Explain that the students will be investigating the properties of potions and identifying five different potions whose labels have got mixed up.

2. For each group, prepare five clear cups, each containing a little of one of the following solutions: plain water; a solution of baking soda and water; white vinegar; lemonade; and ammonia (refer to the table below for details). Don't let the students see you doing this!

3. Give each group a copy of the Revealing Riddle, a set of potions labels and a bottle of Revealing Solution.

4. Instruct them to add a couple of drops of Revealing Solution to each potion and to use the riddle and the results to correctly identify each potion.

The potions and their properties

| LABEL | POTION | SUBSTANCE | COLOUR | ACID/BASE |
|-------|--------|-----------|--------|-----------|
| A | Shrinking Solution | Ammonia | Green | Base |
| B | Ageing Potion | Baking soda solution | Blue | Base |
| C | Veritaserum | Plain water | Purple | Acid |
| D | Draught of Living Death | White vinegar | Red | Acid |
| E | Essence of Gillyweed | Lemonade | Pink | Acid |

! **Alert** ! Instruct students *not* to drink the potions.

## STAGE 2

1. Once all groups have correctly identified all five potions, ask if anyone can identify which scientific concept the activity demonstrates. Depending on the age and prior knowledge of the students, they may be able to recognise that the activity demonstrates acids and bases.

2. Provide all students with some background information on acids and bases and a pH scale. Some basic information is provided on the next page, but you may like to elaborate if the students' existing knowledge and your own familiarity with this topic allow it.

3. Tell the students the identity of the real ingredients and present them with the following challenges:

   – Can you work out which of the potions are acids and which are bases?

   – Now you have this information, can you identify what substance was actually in each of the cups?

   – Using your knowledge of acids and bases, choose one of the potions and write a recipe for it. You should use a combination of real and magical ingredients, and choose acidic or basic ingredients as appropriate.

# Background information

Every liquid you see will probably be either an acid or a base. One exception is distilled water. The positive and negative ions in distilled water are present in equal amounts and cancel each other out. Most tap water has ions in it, which is why the water in our experiment is slightly acidic. It is the ions in a solution that make something acidic or basic. Fruits contain citric acid. Vinegar is another acid. But when baking soda is dissolved in water, it creates a basic solution.

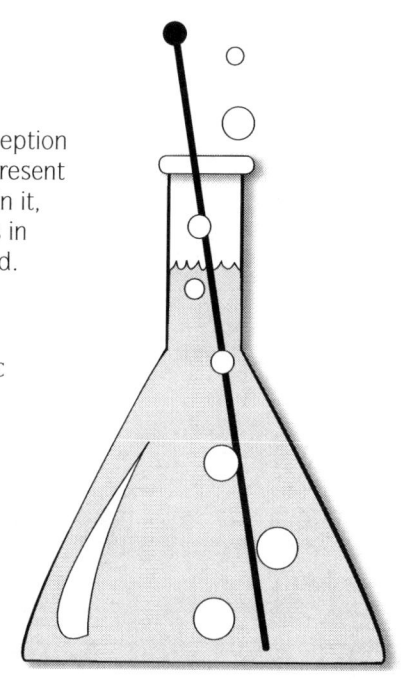

Scientists use the **pH scale** to express how acidic (like an acid) or basic (like a base) a substance is:

☆ A pH value below 7 means that a substance is acidic; the smaller the number, the more acidic the substance is.

☆ A pH value above 7 means that a substance is basic; the larger the number, the more basic the substance is.

☆ A pH value of 7 is neutral.

Adding red cabbage extract to a substance can indicate whether it is an acid (like vinegar) or a base (like ammonia). It can also show how strongly acidic or basic the substance is. Red cabbage has this capacity because it contains water-soluble pigments called **anthocyanins**, which change colour according to whether they are in the presence of an acid or an alkali. The red cabbage extract will turn a particular colour according to the pH value of the substance, as illustrated in the table below.

Colour of red cabbage extract along the pH scale

| APPROXIMATE pH | 2 | 4 | 6 | 8 | 10 | 12 |
|---|---|---|---|---|---|---|
| COLOUR OF EXTRACT | Red | Purple | Violet | Blue | Blue-green | Green |

The pH scale ranges from values very close to 0 up to 14 (see diagram below). Distilled water is 7 (right in the middle). Acids are found between 0 and 7. Bases are from 7 to 14. Most of the common liquids we come into contact with have a pH near 7. It is with the pH of chemicals that the numbers go to the extremes of 1 and 14. There are also very strong acids, such as battery acid, with pH values below 1. Bases with pH values near 14 include drain cleaner and sodium hydroxide (NaOH). Those chemicals are very dangerous.

pH scale

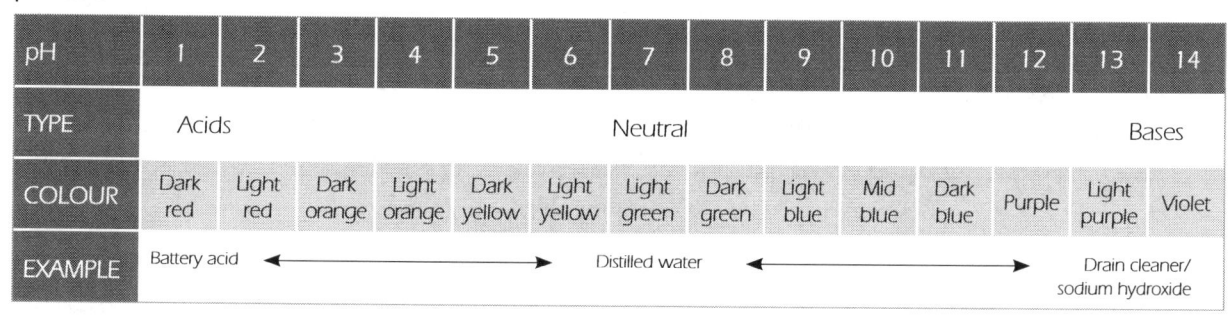

| pH | 1 | 2 | 3 | 4 | 5 | 6 | 7 | 8 | 9 | 10 | 11 | 12 | 13 | 14 |
|---|---|---|---|---|---|---|---|---|---|---|---|---|---|---|
| TYPE | Acids | | | | | | Neutral | | | | | | Bases | |
| COLOUR | Dark red | Light red | Dark orange | Light orange | Dark yellow | Light yellow | Light green | Dark green | Light blue | Mid blue | Dark blue | Purple | Light purple | Violet |
| EXAMPLE | Battery acid ⟵ | | | ⟶ | | Distilled water | | ⟵ | | | ⟶ | | Drain cleaner/ sodium hydroxide | |

# Revealing Riddle

If the truth is what you seek,
Then don't choose pink, it is too weak.
For a tongue you seek to loosen,
Red is not the colour of the solution.

If underwater action is your goal,
The red potion will leave you cold.
Green will leave you feeling small,
It's not the one you want at all.

Asphodel and wormwood together will keep
The drinker in the deepest sleep.
The draught you seek will turn a hue,
But it won't be purple and it won't be blue.

If something you wish to shrink,
Then don't choose red and don't choose pink.
Red will not cause you to age,
Nor will purple, and nor will sage.

Blue might make you grow a beard.
Pink might leave you feeling weird.
Make your choice but heed the clues.
You must be careful which you choose.

Selena Gallagher

# Harry Potter and the hero's journey

## Focus areas

Literacy (writing), critical thinking

## Organisation

Students can work individually, in pairs or in small groups.

## Resources

One copy of **Identifying the hero's journey in** *Harry Potter and the Philosopher's Stone* (page 16), for each student, pair or group

> This activity introduces the powerful concept of the hero's journey to develop a deeper understanding of Harry Potter's story and to indicate how it can be applied more widely in literature and films.

## What to do

1. Introduce the topic of this activity with a whole-group discussion:
   - Ask students if they can identify any similarities between Harry Potter's journey and those of other fictional heroes from books or films (eg, Luke Skywalker from *Star Wars*).
   - Explain the concept of the hero's journey, as described by Joseph Campbell and Christopher Vogler (see background information on the following page).
   - Explain and discuss each stage of the hero's journey, seeking lots of examples from popular culture, literature and films.

2. As a whole group, discuss *Harry Potter and the Philosopher's Stone* in terms of the hero's journey. Find an example for each stage from the book. Some suggestions are provided, but these are open to individual interpretation. Students can use the **Identifying the hero's journey** information to note down the group-generated suggestions, or a master record can be made on an interactive whiteboard or similar.

3. Ask students, preferably in pairs or small groups, to consider one other book in the Harry Potter series and complete the exercise, finding an example for each stage from their chosen book.

4. As a whole group, share and discuss each group's responses. Ensure students recognise that while elements of the hero's journey can be seen in each volume of the Harry Potter series, the model can also be applied to the series as a whole.

5. You could discuss whether J.K. Rowling consciously used the hero's journey template to guide her writing, or whether the story just naturally evolved to follow that pattern. After all, early myths such as those of Hercules and Achilles certainly were not written to a formula, but they still follow a common pattern. Within the Harry Potter novels, certain elements appear to emerge very strongly, such as the way the story always begins in the ordinary world. Stage 7, "Approaching the innermost cave", was traditionally a descent into the underworld or an entry into the land of the dead. Consider the location of the climactic scenes in at least the first five Harry Potter novels:
   - in *Philosopher's Stone*, Harry goes through the trapdoor and descends into a hidden area
   - in *Chamber of Secrets*, the climax takes place in a hidden chamber deep under the school
   - in *Prisoner of Azkaban*, the protagonists go along an underground tunnel to the Shrieking Shack
   - *Goblet of Fire* stays above ground, but in a graveyard, definitely a land of the dead
   - *Order of the Phoenix* descends into the bowels of the Ministry of Magic, again underground.

The final two novels deviate from this pattern, with the action taking place on top of the astronomy tower, and in the Hogwarts grounds and forest. Students may like to discuss these patterns and their impact, or possible reasons for altering the established pattern.

**Possible extension activity**: Students could use the hero's journey model to develop their own work of fiction.

---

# Background information

Joseph Campbell was an American mythologist who studied myths and legends from around the world. He recognised that they followed a familiar pattern, which he described as the **hero's journey**. Later, Christopher Vogler took Campbell's hero's journey structure and revised it, simplifying it a little and referring to it as the **writer's journey**.

The best-known and best-remembered stories follow this pattern, from ancient myths through to more modern-day fables including, of course, the Harry Potter series. The steps on the following page are those described by Vogler (1992), presenting a more useful and user-friendly model to use with students than Campbell's original version.

After reading through the activity, discuss how the hero's journey applies to the examples listed below. Add any others you can think of, with the exception of the Harry Potter series, which is the focus of the next activity.

Examples of the hero's journey

| STORY | HERO | ELEMENTS OF THE HERO'S JOURNEY |
|---|---|---|
| The Labours of Hercules | Hercules | |
| The Odyssey | Odysseus | |
| The Iliad | Achilles | |
| The Legends of King Arthur | King Arthur | |
| The Lord of the Rings | Frodo Baggins | |
| The Adventures of Robin Hood | Robin Hood | |
| The Lion King | Simba | |
| Star Wars IV–VI | Luke Skywalker | |
| | | |
| | | |

Overview of the hero's journey

1. **Ordinary world**: The story starts in the ordinary world with the hero going about their everyday existence, oblivious of the adventures to come. This context anchors the hero as a human, just like you and me, which helps us to identify with them.

2. **Call to adventure**: Something shakes up the situation, from either external or internal pressures. The hero must face the beginnings of change.

3. **Refusal of the call**: The hero feels the fear of the unknown and tries to turn away from the adventure, however briefly. Alternatively, another character may express a sense of the uncertainty and danger ahead.

4. **Meeting the mentor**: The mentor appears to help the hero prepare for the road ahead. Thus Gandalf, Obi-wan Kenobi, Dumbledore or other wise and experienced people teach the hero the skills they need and give them essential knowledge to help them survive.

5. **Crossing the threshold**: Eventually the hero is ready to act and crosses the threshold, often literally, as they leave the safety of home to begin their journey into the unknown.

6. **Tests, allies, enemies**: The hero is confronted with an ever more difficult series of challenges, ranging from minor skirmishes and struggles against weather and terrain to riddles and various setbacks that would defeat a lesser person. In this way the hero's character is both highlighted and developed.

7. **Approaching the innermost cave**: The hero approaches the final destination, battered but wiser from their trials along the way. They must prepare for the ultimate test. In ancient legend, a typical "innermost cave" is the land of the dead or a labyrinth. It is the lair of the dreaded enemy where no help may be found and only deep courage will win through. Another threshold must be crossed here to enter the innermost cave.

8. **Ordeal**: At last the hero must face their deepest fears, typically in battle with the dark villain. This is the ultimate test that the hero takes; the real story perhaps is the inner battle whereby the hero overcomes their own demons in facing up to the enemy outside.

9. **Reward (seizing the sword)**: In defeating the enemy, the hero is transformed into a new state where fears are vanquished and the new fearless person is born. The reward in the story may be gaining new knowledge or a treasure or rescuing a princess, but the inner reward is in the personal growth that is achieved.

10. **The road back**: After the story has reached its main peak, the transformed hero sets out for home again. Having gained the treasure they have no need for more adventure and nothing left to prove. Setting out for home is a reverse echo of crossing the threshold at the beginning of the adventure. In contrast to the earlier anticipation of danger, the anticipation now is of acclaim and rest.

11. **Resurrection**: The story has one last trick up its sleeve. Having lulled its audience into a false sense of security, one last challenge faces the hero. Perhaps the villain was not completely vanquished or perhaps there are other people in need on the way back – whichever way, we are again plunged into another climactic event, just when we thought it was safe to breathe easy again.

12. **Return with the elixir**: Finally, the hero returns to the hero's welcome, gives the treasure to the proper recipient and receives their just reward, whether it is the hand of the princess, the acclaim of the people or simply a well-deserved rest. In this final part, all tensions are resolved and all previously unanswered questions answered, leaving the reader of the story satisfied and replete.

**Source: Adapted from Vogler (1992)**

Identifying the hero's journey in *Harry Potter and the Philosopher's Stone*

| STAGE OF THE JOURNEY | EXAMPLE(S) FROM THE BOOK |
| --- | --- |
| Ordinary world | |
| Call to adventure | |
| Refusal of the call | |
| Meeting the mentor | |
| Crossing the threshold | |
| Tests, allies, enemies | |
| Approaching the innermost cave | |
| Ordeal | |
| Reward (seizing the sword) | |
| The road back | |
| Resurrection | |
| Return with the elixir | |

SAMPLE ANSWERS

Identifying the hero's journey in *Harry Potter and the Philosopher's Stone*

| STAGE OF THE JOURNEY | EXAMPLE(S) FROM THE BOOK |
|---|---|
| Ordinary world | 4 Privet Drive, life with the Dursleys |
| Call to adventure | The letters start to arrive |
| Refusal of the call | Here it's not Harry who is refusing but Vernon, who does everything he can to stop Harry getting the letters |
| Meeting the mentor | The main mentor in the series is Dumbledore, but he sometimes acts through others. Here it's Hagrid at the Hut on the Rock |
| Crossing the threshold | The physical threshold at Kings Cross. Also the magical threshold into Diagon Alley |
| Tests, allies, enemies | Tests – troll, Norbert, Quidditch |
| Allies | Ron & Hermione |
| Enemies | Malfoy & Snape |
| Approaching the innermost cave | Descending through the trapdoor and navigating the series of challenges guarding the stone |
| Ordeal | Facing Professor Quirrel and Voldemort (in the back of Quirrel's head!) |
| Reward (seizing the sword) | Obtaining the Philosopher's Stone |
| The road back | Waking up in the hospital wing. Debriefing with Dumbledore |
| Resurrection | We learn the danger is not past, Voldemort will return |
| Return with the elixir | Harry and friends receive enough house points to win the House Cup for Gryffindor |

# Anagrams never lie

## Focus areas

Literacy (reading), problem solving

## Organisation

This activity works well with a group, with an element of competition, but could also be done individually.

## Resources

One copy of **Decoding anagrams** (page 19), for each student
Copies of the **Cheat sheet** (page 19) (optional)

## Recommended anagram websites

| Internet Anagram Server | wordsmith.org/anagram |
| --- | --- |
| Anagram Genius | www.anagramgenius.com/ |

**TOM MARVOLO RIDDLE becomes I AM LORD VOLDEMORT**

*With this example revealed in* Chamber of Secrets, *J.K. Rowling herself opened up the never-ending possibilities of hidden meanings within the books. While fans of the series eagerly waited for each new instalment, fan websites were a hive of discussion covering theories about what might happen next and what seemingly fleeting incident might be a clue to future storylines. For example, when Neville visits his parents in the closed ward at St Mungo's, his mother presses a Droobles Best Blowing Gum wrapper into his hand. Rearranging the letters in* Droobles Best Blowing Gum *gives you* Gold bribe below St Mungo's *which led to a complicated theory suggesting that Neville's parents weren't really insane but were being deliberately kept in that state by some evil plot! That idea turned out to be incorrect, but it was a lot of fun speculating.*

## What to do

1. Discuss J.K. Rowling's use of anagrams and other plays on words in the Harry Potter series. Even in the first book, there are hints at deeper meanings with the Mirror of Erised and in the geographical names Diagon Alley and Knockturn Alley. (Have students noticed what is special about each of these three examples?) **Decoding anagrams** provides some additional examples you could discuss as a class.

2. Hand out copies of **Decoding anagrams** and challenge the students to solve the anagrams on it. To introduce an element of competition, set individuals or groups the challenge of being the first to solve all 10 anagrams.

   Students may need a reminder of some lesser-known characters in order to solve all of the anagrams. After the students have solved as many as possible on their own, you may choose to give them the **Cheat sheet** which lists all 10 solutions among a longer list of possible answers.

   After solving the anagrams, students may like to share their successful strategies.

3. Can students think of any other examples of books, games or films where anagrams are used? Possible examples are the *Deltora Quest* books and *The Da Vinci Code* book and film.

4. Challenge students to make an anagram using their own name. Students might use an internet anagram server to help with suggestions (see some possible websites above). Imagine my surprise to discover that my name anagrams to Her Legal Lasagne!

5. As a variation on the above, students can rearrange the letters in their name to make an alias – perhaps a more wizardy sounding name that could be used as a character in a fantasy story. My wizardy anagram name is Helga Sallagreen.

## Decoding anagrams

Here are some examples of anagrams connected to the Harry Potter books:

**TOM MARVOLO RIDDLE** becomes **I AM LORD VOLDEMORT**

Think about what happens in the first chapter of *Goblet of Fire*. Is it any wonder that the chapter title is an anagram?

**THE RIDDLE HOUSE** becomes **THREE SHOULD DIE**

And how's this for spooky? The director of the fourth film was Mike Newell, so it could be referred to as:

**MIKE NEWELL'S HARRY POTTER AND THE GOBLET OF FIRE**
which becomes

**ENTHRALLING FILM, YET WE PREFER TO READ THE BOOKS**

Listed below are some anagrams formed from characters' names. In most cases the anagram also provides a clue to the character's identity. See how many you can solve.

1. AN EVIL LORD _____
2. TRY HERO PART _____
3. EVIL MEN MENACE _____
4. BLAMED OLD RUBEUS _____
5. DUMBLEDORE GOES IN JAR _____
6. SAVE PURENESS _____
7. TIP: PET WE REGRET _____
8. WE SALUTE HARRY _____
9. MAN SO HATED _____
10. ON HAND TO MARK SPY _____

- - - - - - - - - - - - - - - - - - - - - - - - - - - - - - - ✂ - -

## Cheat sheet for resource sheet: Decoding anagrams

The anagrams match 10 of the characters named here.

| | |
|---|---|
| HARRY POTTER | ALBUS DUMBLEDORE |
| RUBEUS HAGRID | ARTHUR WEASLEY |
| RON WEASLEY | MINERVA MCGONAGALL |
| PETER PETTIGREW | MOLLY WEASLEY |
| HERMIONE GRANGER | SEVERUS SNAPE |
| NYMPHADORA TONKS | BARTY CROUCH |
| SEAMUS FINNIGAN | REMUS LUPIN |
| KINGSLEY SHACKLEBOLT | FLOREAN FORTESCUE |
| DEAN THOMAS | LUDO BAGMAN |
| EMMELINE VANCE | OLLIVANDER |
| NEVILLE LONGBOTTOM | RITA SKEETER |
| DOLORES JANE UMBRIDGE | DEDALUS DIGGLE |

### Answers

1. OLLIVANDER, 2. HARRY POTTER, 3. EMMELINE VANCE, 4. ALBUS DUMBLEDORE, 5. DOLORES JANE UMBRIDGE, 6. SEVERUS SNAPE, 7. PETER PETTIGREW, 8. ARTHUR WEASLEY, 9. DEAN THOMAS, 10. NYMPHADORA TONKS

# What's in a name?

## Focus areas

Literacy (reading), creative thinking

## Organisation

Students can work individually, in pairs or in small groups.

## Resources

One copy of **A new middle name** (page 21), for each student
Selection of mythology books
Latin dictionary
Good English dictionaries and thesauruses

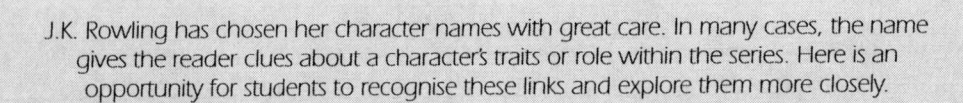

J.K. Rowling has chosen her character names with great care. In many cases, the name gives the reader clues about a character's traits or role within the series. Here is an opportunity for students to recognise these links and explore them more closely.

## What to do

1. Discuss with students some of the character names from the Harry Potter series. Can they explain the meaning behind some of them? Some are discussed in **A new middle name**, but the following are others the students may be aware of.

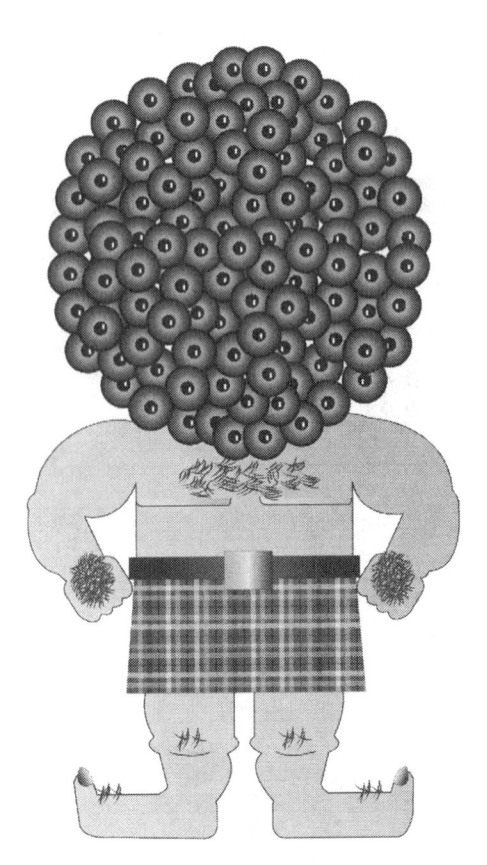

| NAME | ASSOCIATIONS |
| --- | --- |
| Albus | White |
| Hermes (Percy's owl) | Greek god, messenger to Zeus |
| Argus (Filch) | From Greek mythology, giant with 100 eyes |
| Lucius (Malfoy) | Associated with Lucifer or Satan |
| Narcissa (Malfoy) | From Greek mythology, Narcissus fell in love with his own reflection; narcissistic |

2. Hand out copies of **A new middle name** and discuss the character names that are listed there.

3. Based on what they know about the characters, students should choose a new middle name for each of the characters listed. They can use the mythology books provided for inspiration.

---

## A new middle name

Here are some examples of character names and their possible meanings. Using what you know about each character, create a new middle name to suit them.

The star Sirius (also known as the Dog Star) is the brightest star in the sky. Celestial names seem to have been a tradition in the Black household – many others in the family, including Regulus and Andromeda, are also named after constellations.

The colour black has many associations.

From Roman mythology, Remus was raised along with his twin brother Romulus by a she-wolf. The twin element may also refer to Lupin's dual nature: he is both man and wolf.

The Latin *lupus* means "wolf". A person who looks wolf-like is said to be *lupine*.

Minerva is the Roman goddess of wisdom.

This Scottish name comes from the Celtic *conegal* which means "the bravest".

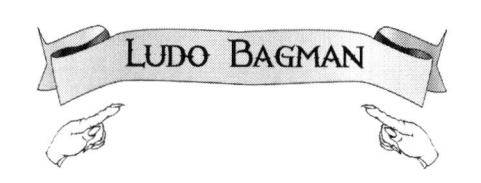

The Latin word *ludo* means "I play".

A bagman collects money for racketeers or is a travelling salesman.

*Draco* is Latin for "dragon"

*Mal* is the Latin root for "bad" – think about *malevolent* or *malignant*. In French, *mal foi* means "bad faith".

| FIRST NAME | MIDDLE NAME (NEW) | FAMILY NAME |
|---|---|---|
| Sirius | | Black |
| Remus | | Lupin |
| Minerva | | McGonagall |
| Ludo | | Bagman |
| Draco | | Malfoy |

# How well can you spell?

## Focus areas

Literacy (reading), creative thinking

## Organisation

Students can work individually, in pairs or in small groups.

## Resources

One copy of **Some spells and their etymology** (page 23), for each student
Latin (plus possibly Spanish and Italian) dictionaries
Good English dictionaries and thesauruses

As with her character names, J.K. Rowling has created magic words for her spells with great care and skill.
If Harry had had even the most basic grounding in Latin, there is no way he
would have used *Sectumsempra* on Draco Malfoy in the bathroom in *Half Blood Prince*.
Many but not all of the spells in the series have their roots in Latin, as students
will become more aware of in completing this activity.

## What to do

1. Give out copies of **Some spells and their etymology**, and discuss the examples of spells and their etymologies listed. How many are they already aware of?

2. Challenge students to create three (or more) original spells. They should provide the magic word, clearly describe what the spell does, and explain the etymology of the spell. Provide a selection of Latin dictionaries for students to browse through for inspiration. Italian or Spanish dictionaries may also be helpful if you can't find a Latin dictionary or if you only have one and are working with a larger group of students. Good English dictionaries are also invaluable.

**Possible extension:** Students could write a short vignette in which a Harry Potter character uses one or more of the students' invented spells.

Some spells and their etymology

| MAGIC WORD | PURPOSE OF SPELL | ETYMOLOGY OF MAGIC WORD |
|---|---|---|
| *Accio* | Summoning charm | Means "to send for" or "to summon" in Latin. |
| *Alohamora* | Open locks | Derived from the Hawaiian word *aloha*, meaning "goodbye" (as well as "hello"), and the Latin word *mora*, meaning "obstacle". So literally, "goodbye obstacle". |
| *Crucio* | Torture | Latin for "I torture". Think about the word *excruciating*. |
| *Expecto patronum* | Banish Dementors | In Latin, *expecto* is "to await, desire or hope for" and *patronus* means "protector". |
| *Incendio* | Create fire | From the Latin *incendere*, which means "to set fire to". *Incendio* is also Spanish for "great fire". Think about the word *incendiary*. |
| *Levicorpus* (*Liberacorpus* counter-curse) | Suspend someone in mid air; counter-curse reverses the spell | In Latin *levi* means "to raise" and *corpus* means "body". *Libera* is Latin for "to free". Think about *levitate* and *liberate*. |
| *Lumos* | Light up the end of the wand | Derived from *lumen*, which is Latin for "light". Think about *illuminate* and *luminous*. |
| *Obliviate* | Erase someone's memory | Possibly a combination of the words *obliterate*, which means to wipe out, erase or remove all traces, and *oblivious* meaning forgetful or unaware. |
| *Sectumsempra* | Cause serious wounds | In Latin, *sectum* means "to cut, wound or amputate" and *sempra* is derived from *semper*, meaning "always, at all times". |

Now write three spells of your own in the table below.

| MAGIC WORD | PURPOSE OF SPELL | ETYMOLOGY (TO EXPLAIN YOUR CHOICE OF MAGIC WORD) |
|---|---|---|
|  |  |  |
|  |  |  |
|  |  |  |

# What's your Boggart?

## Focus areas

Drama, critical thinking

## Organisation

Students work in a larger group divided into at least two teams.

## Resources

A set of **Worst-fear cards** – make your own, with one card for each fear listed on pages 25–26 and cut out individually (you can create more cards with the names of particularly scary characters from the series if you wish)
A timer – large egg timer or similar

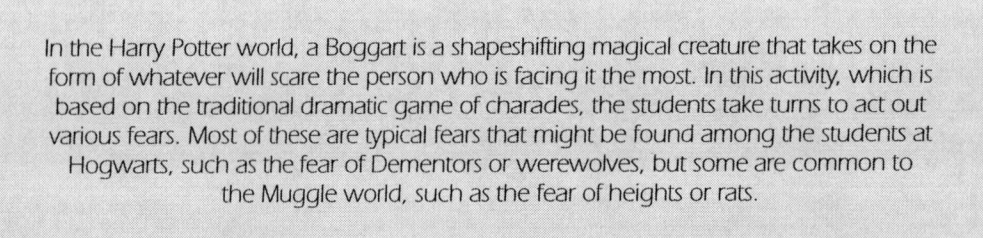

In the Harry Potter world, a Boggart is a shapeshifting magical creature that takes on the form of whatever will scare the person who is facing it the most. In this activity, which is based on the traditional dramatic game of charades, the students take turns to act out various fears. Most of these are typical fears that might be found among the students at Hogwarts, such as the fear of Dementors or werewolves, but some are common to the Muggle world, such as the fear of heights or rats.

## What to do

1. Organise the students into teams, or houses, for the game. Then follow these steps to play the game:
   - A student from one team chooses a Worst-fear card at random from the pile and acts out whatever Boggart is on the card. The usual rules of charades apply, in that the student may not speak, but must rely on their miming skills.
   - With the timer set for one minute, the student's own team has up to one minute to correctly identify the Boggart. No other team can guess during the first minute.
   - If the student's team cannot guess the Boggart during the first minute, the student continues to mime, but any team can now guess. The team that correctly guesses the Boggart gets a point.
   - The game continues in this way, with teams taking turns to act out the Boggarts, and all students having a turn.

2. Following the game, lead the students in a group discussion about the nature of fear. You could consider questions such as:
   - Does all fear have a physical appearance?
   - What shape would the Boggart take on to represent a fear of the unknown, or the fear of not being perfect?
   - Lupin said that what Harry feared was fear itself, and that this was wise. What did he mean?

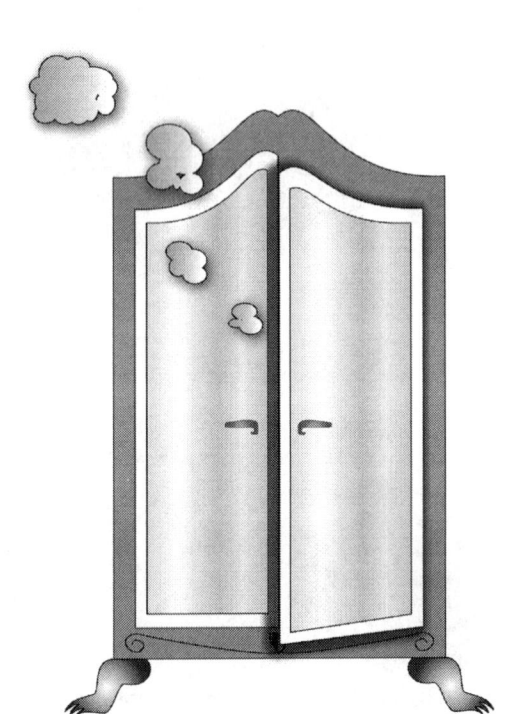

**Possible extension activity:** Students could write a personal journal entry describing their own fears. They may or may not choose to share it with the teacher, but should be encouraged to write it nevertheless.

Fears to use for your own set of Worst-fear cards

Create one card for each fear listed here. You can create more cards with names of particularly scary characters from the series too if you wish.

**Mummy**

**Vampire**

**Centaur**

**Giants**

**The scariest teacher at school**

**Pixies**

**Dragon**

**Being buried alive**

**Werewolf**

**Heights**

Fears to use for your own set of Worst-fear cards
Create one card for each fear listed here.

A meat-eating flying horse

Banshee

Clowns

Basilisk

Failure

Grim reaper

A lord who is too terrifying to name

Life-sucking prison guards

An enormous, venomous spider

Rats

# Hagrid's experimental breeding programme

## Focus areas

Visual art, creative thinking

## Organisation

Students can work individually or in pairs.

## Resources

Cards created based on the ideas summarised in the **Creature information notes** (pages 28–29), cut out individually – enough for each student or pair to use two or three
Art supplies

> "I can certainly see why we're trying to keep them alive. Who wouldn't want pets that can burn, sting and bite all at once?"
>
> Draco Malfoy,
> *Harry Potter and the Goblet of Fire*, Chapter 13
>
> Who could forget the Blast-Ended Skrewts? These were the result of Hagrid's breeding experiment and were a cross between Manticores and Fire-Crabs. The result was a ferocious, ugly creature that almost defies description – a kind of cross between a giant scorpion and an elongated crab that, as Draco points out, could burn, sting and bite all at once.
>
> The premise behind this activity is that Hagrid has not been put off by his first attempt at creating a new species, but is determined to try again.

## What to do

1. Discuss the Blast-Ended Skrewt example with the students and explain that their job is to help Hagrid create a new species of magical creature.

2. Read and discuss the creature descriptions on the creature cards you have created. Some of these magical creatures feature in the Harry Potter books, but some of them can only be found in J.K. Rowling's companion book, *Fantastic Beasts and Where to Find Them*.

3. Ask the students to choose a maximum of three different creatures to virtually interbreed in order to create a new species of magical creature. They are to create a visual representation of their creature by drawing, painting or using any other artistic technique of your choice, for which you have the necessary supplies.

   In addition to their picture, students should write the following information about their creature:
   – the name of the new species
   – the creatures that have been combined to create it
   – its appearance
   – its eating habits, diet etc
   – its sleeping habits
   – its behaviour
   – any other relevant information.

Creature information notes

## CRUP

The Crup originated in the southeast of England. It closely resembles a Jack Russell terrier, except that it has a forked tail. The Crup is almost certainly a wizard-created dog, as it is intensely loyal to wizards and ferocious towards Muggles. It is a great scavenger, eating anything from gnomes to old tyres.

Crup licences may be obtained from the department for the regulation and control of magical creatures on completion of a simple test to prove that the applicant wizard is capable of controlling the crup in muggle-inhabited areas. Crup owners are legally obliged to remove the crup's tail with a painless severing charm while the crup is six to eight weeks old, lest muggles notice it.

## DIRICAWL

The Diricawl originated in Mauritius. A plump-bodied, fluffy-feathered, flightless bird, the Diricawl is remarkable for its method of escaping danger. It can vanish in a puff of feathers and reappear elsewhere (the phoenix shares this ability).

Interestingly, Muggles were once fully aware of the existence of the Diricawl, though they knew it by the name of "dodo". Unaware that the Diricawl can vanish at will, Muggles believe they have hunted the species to extinction. As this belief seems to have raised Muggle awareness of the dangers of slaying their fellow creatures indiscriminately, the International Confederation of Wizards has never deemed it appropriate that the Muggles should be made aware of the continued existence of the Diricawl.

## KNEAZLE

The Kneazle was originally bred in Britain, though it is now exported worldwide. A small, cat-like creature with flecked, speckled or spotted fur, outsized ears and a tail like a lion's, the Kneazle is intelligent, independent and occasionally aggressive, though if it takes a liking to a witch or wizard, it makes an excellent pet. The Kneazle has an uncanny ability to detect unsavoury or suspicious characters and can be relied upon to guide its owner safely home if they are lost. Kneazles have up to eight kittens in a litter and can interbreed with cats.

Licences are required for ownership as (like Crups and Fwoopers) Kneazles are sufficiently unusual in appearance to attract Muggle interest.

## FWOOPER

The Fwooper is an African bird with extremely vivid plumage; Fwoopers may be orange, pink, lime green or yellow. The Fwooper has long been a provider of fancy quills and also lays brilliantly patterned eggs. Though at first enjoyable, Fwooper song will eventually drive the listener to insanity* and the Fwooper is consequently sold with a Silencing Charm upon it, which will need monthly reinforcement.

Fwooper owners require licences, as the creatures must be handled responsibly.

* Uric the Oddball attempted at one time to prove that Fwooper song was actually beneficial to the health and listened to it for three months on end without a break. Unfortunately, the Wizards' Council to which he reported his findings was unconvinced, as he had arrived at the meeting wearing nothing but a toupee that on closer inspection proved to be a dead badger.

Source: *Fantastic Beasts and Where to Find Them* © J.K. Rowling 2001

Creature information notes *continued*

## NIFFLER

The Niffler is a British beast. Fluffy, black and long-snouted, this burrowing creature has a predilection for anything glittery. Nifflers are often kept by goblins to burrow deep into the earth for treasure. Though the Niffler is gentle and even affectionate, it can be destructive to belongings and should never be kept in a house. Nifflers live in lairs up to 6 metres below the surface and produce six to eight young in a litter.

## DOXY

The Doxy is often mistaken for a fairy though it is a quite separate species. Like the fairy, it has a minute human form, but in the Doxy's case this is covered in thick black hair and has an extra pair of arms and legs. The Doxy's wings are thick, curved and shiny, much like a beetle's. Doxies are found throughout Northern Europe and America, preferring cold climates. They lay up to 500 eggs at a time and bury them. The eggs hatch in two to three weeks.

Doxies have double rows of sharp, venomous teeth. An antidote should be taken if bitten by one.

## PUFFSKEIN

The Puffskein is found worldwide. Spherical in shape and covered in soft, custard-coloured fur, it is a docile creature that has no objection to being cuddled or thrown about. Easy to care for, it emits a low humming noise when contented. From time to time a very long, thin, pink tongue will emerge from the depths of the Puffskein and snake through the house searching for food.

The Puffskein is a scavenger that will eat anything from leftovers to spiders, but it has a particular preference for sticking its tongue up the nose of sleeping wizards and eating their bogies. This tendency has made the Puffskein much beloved by wizarding children for many generations and it remains a highly popular wizarding pet.

## CLABBERT

The Clabbert is a tree-dwelling creature, in appearance something like a cross between a monkey and a frog. It originated in the southern states of the USA, though it has since been exported worldwide. The smooth and hairless skin is a mottled green, the hands and feet are webbed, and the arms and legs are long and supple, enabling the Clabbert to swing between branches with the agility of an orang-utan. The head has short horns, and the wide mouth, which appears to be grinning, is full of razor-sharp teeth. The Clabbert feeds mostly on small lizards and birds.

The Clabbert's most distinctive feature is the large pustule in the middle of its forehead, which turns scarlet and flashes when it senses danger. American wizards once kept Clabberts in their gardens to give early warning of approaching Muggles, but the International Confederation of Wizards has introduced fines which have largely ended this practice. The sight of a tree at night full of glowing Clabbert pustules, while decorative, attracted too many Muggles asking why their neighbours still had their Christmas lights up in June.

Source: *Fantastic Beasts and Where to Find Them* © J.K. Rowling 2001

# A potty perspective

## Focus area

Literacy (writing)

## Organisation

Students work individually.

## Resources

Copies of the Harry Potter books, or of extracts from them

Cards created based on the **Scenario information notes** (page 31), cut out individually – the number depends on the approach you choose to take for this activity (see below)

One or more copies of the **Rewriting activity guidelines and planning sheet** (page 32)

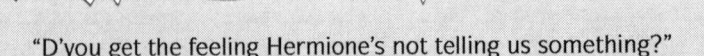

> **"D'you get the feeling Hermione's not telling us something?"**
>
> Ron asking Harry,
> *Harry Potter and the Prisoner of Azkaban*, Chapter 7
>
> J.K. Rowling is a master of the red herring, the surprise twist and the unexpected ending. She is able to keep us guessing throughout the series, in large part because of the **narrative** voice that she uses to tell the story. With the exception of the first chapters of *Goblet of Fire*, *Half-Blood Prince* and *Deathly Hallows*, the story is told from Harry's perspective. As a reader, for the most part, we know only what Harry knows, and sometimes that's not much. However, the story is not written in the first person, which gives us a slightly wider perspective than we would get if we were limited to Harry's narration.
>
> The narrative voice J.K. Rowling uses is a variation of third person, called **limited omniscient**. This voice helps us to feel emotionally connected to Harry, but still allows the author to maintain the air of mystery necessary to keep readers guessing.
>
> For this activity, students will experiment with the effect of perspective by rewriting scenes from the book from the perspective of another character.

## What to do

1. Discuss with students the effect of using different perspectives. Compare the effects of using the first person and the third person in particular.

2. The approach you choose to take to the rewriting activity may depend on the size and ability level of the group you are working with. For example, you might:
   - select one of the scenarios and jointly construct a text as a group, before students choose a different scenario to work on independently
   - ask all the students to independently work on the same scenario, then come together to share their versions and discuss tips and strategies, before choosing a different scenario to work on individually
   - ask all the students to work on a scenario of their own choice, initially choosing from one of those on the scenario cards, before moving on to a self-selected piece of their own.

3. According to the approach you have chosen, students rewrite one of the scenarios from the scenario cards you have created (referring for further detail to the Harry Potter books or extracts you have available) from a different perspective. Discuss the **Rewriting activity guidelines and planning sheet**. Hand out copies for students to refer to and use for planning their rewritten version.

Scenario information notes

## Harry Potter and the Philosopher's Stone        Chapter 17: The Man with Two Faces

**Scenario**: At the end of the chapter, Harry enters the Great Hall for the end-of-term assembly, Dumbledore awards the last-minute points and Gryffindor wins the House Cup.

**Perspective**: Rewrite this scene from the perspective of Draco Malfoy.

## Harry Potter and the Chamber of Secrets        Chapter 2: Dobby's Warning

**Scenario**: In Harry's bedroom, Dobby arrives to try to persuade Harry not to return to Hogwarts, culminating in the "pudding incident".

**Perspective**: Rewrite this scene from the perspective of Dobby.

## Harry Potter and the Prisoner of Azkaban        Chapter 4: The Leaky Cauldron

**Scenario**: Harry, Ron and Hermione enter the Magical Menagerie, a pet shop in Diagon Alley, as Ron wants to find something to make Scabbers healthier. Hermione buys Crookshanks.

**Perspective**: Rewrite this scene from the perspective of Crookshanks.

## Harry Potter and the Goblet of Fire        Chapter 23: The Yule Ball

**Scenario**: Hermione surprises everyone as she arrives at the Yule Ball with her date, Viktor Krum. Ron accuses her of "consorting with the enemy" and they end the evening by having a blazing argument.

**Perspective**: Rewrite this scene from the perspective of Hermione.

## Harry Potter and the Order of the Phoenix        Chapter 1: Dudley Demented

**Scenario**: Harry joins Dudley as they walk home from the park, and after exchanging some banter the pair are set upon by two Dementors. Harry fights them off and, with Mrs Figg's help, gets Dudley home.

**Perspective**: Rewrite this scene from the perspective of Dudley.

## Harry Potter and the Half-Blood Prince        Chapter 13: The Secret Riddle

**Scenario**: In the pensieve, we see Dumbledore's visit to the Muggle orphanage where Voldemort spent his childhood. Dumbledore meets Tom Riddle, tells him he is a wizard and invites him to Hogwarts.

**Perspective**: Rewrite this scene from the perspective of Tom Riddle.

## Harry Potter and the Deathly Hallows        Chapter 19: The Silver Doe

**Scenario**: Harry dives into the frozen pool to retrieve the sword of Gryffindor but is nearly choked by the locket horcrux. He is saved by Ron who has returned after being guided by the Deluminator. Harry opens the horcrux and Ron destroys it.

**Perspective**: Rewrite this scene from the perspective of Ron.

☆ You may choose to write in the first person or the third person, but it must be from the perspective of the specified character.

☆ Only write about what the character will be able to see and hear. For example, at the leaving feast in *Philosopher's Stone*, Draco would not be able to hear any of the conversation that might be going on at the Gryffindor table, but he would still hear Dumbledore's speech as it was reported in the book.

☆ In the above example, although Draco would still be able to hear Dumbledore's speech, does that mean that you have to just copy those sections word for word from the book? What other approaches could you use to convey the information?

☆ Think about what the character will know about and what they won't. For example, when Harry, Ron and Hermione enter the Magical Menagerie, Crookshanks won't know their names or who they are. How would Crookshanks refer to the trio?

☆ Plan the key elements of your new version of the scenario in the space below.

## Rewriting plan

Scenario: _____

Perspective: _____

Key features of rewritten version:

# Ordinary Wizarding Levels (practice questions)

## Focus area

Creative thinking

## Organisation

Students work in small groups.

## Resources

Copies of the **OWL practice questions** (page 34)
Imagination!

> All students at Hogwarts take Ordinary Wizarding Levels (OWLs) in their fifth year, followed by Nastily Exhausting Wizarding Tests (NEWTs) in their seventh year.
>
> This activity includes a number of questions that might appear on these tests. To answer them, however, students should rely on creativity and imagination rather than hours of Hermione-enforced revision.

## What to do

You may choose to present individual practice questions for a quick creative thinking exercise, or all three of them together for a longer session.

## Teaching notes on answering the questions

For the first two questions, which are not to be taken too seriously, students should simply be encouraged to give free rein to their imagination and to exercise their sense of humour. The third question requires a more evidence-based response.

☆ **Question 1**: The sky is the limit here. Students should be encouraged to come up with as many divergent responses as possible. Answers could vary from "an essential ingredient in toothpaste for vampires" to "a powerful oven cleaner".

☆ **Question 2**: Again, imagination and creativity are the key ingredients. Possible responses include:
Is a great keeper in Quidditch, but only catches the quaffle with his mouth.
Walks in a circle around his bed three times before going to sleep at night.
Doesn't own a towel; he dries off with a vigorous shake after a shower.

☆ **Question 3**: Although imagination and creativity are still essential elements, students must consider the question more carefully in light of information presented in the series and justify their choices by presenting supporting evidence. An obvious exception to choose may be money; we can point to evidence that wizards cannot simply conjure money out of thin air – for example, the Weasleys are cash-strapped and the leprechaun gold that rains down on the spectators at the Quidditch World Cup disappears after a few hours. However, what ideas and evidence will students come up with?

# Question 1: The 12 uses of dragon's blood

ALBUS DUMBLEDORE, currently Headmaster of Hogwarts

Considered by many the greatest wizard of modern times, Dumbledore is particularly famous for his defeat of the dark wizard Grindelwald in 1945, for the discovery of the 12 uses of dragon's blood, and his work on alchemy with his partner, Nicholas Flamel.

Professor Dumbledore enjoys chamber music and tenpin bowling.

Chocolate Frog Card,
*Harry Potter and the Philosopher's Stone*, Chapter 6

List the 12 uses of dragon's blood.

# Question 2: The top five ways to spot a werewolf

" 'Give five signs that identify the werewolf.' Excellent question ... One: He's sitting on my chair. Two: He's wearing my clothes. Three: His name's Remus Lupin ..."

Lupin discussing the Defence Against the Dark Arts OWL he has just sat,
*Harry Potter and the Order of the Phoenix*, Chapter 28

What are the top five ways to spot a werewolf?

# Question 3: Gamp's Law of Elemental Transfiguration

"My mother," said Ron ..., "can make good food appear out of thin air."

"Your mother can't produce food out of thin air," said Hermione. "No one can. Food is the first of the five Principal Exceptions to Gamp's Law of Elemental Transfigura—"

"Oh, speak English, can't you?"

Ron and Hermione while on the run in Wales,
*Harry Potter and the Deathly Hallows*, Chapter 7

If food is the first of the five Principal Exceptions to Gamp's Law of Elemental Transfiguration, what are the other four exceptions? Justify your answers. Continue on the back of this sheet if you need to.

# Wingardium Leviosa (the levitation challenge)

## Focus areas

Creative thinking, problem solving

## Organisation

Students work in small groups.

## Resources

One bag or tray per group, each of which contains the same selection of items. Each must contain one large feather or preferably two (artificial ones are available from craft shops), plus a range of other items such as:

☆ balloons
☆ paper clips
☆ string
☆ assorted magnets
☆ stiff card
☆ straws
☆ elastic bands
☆ plastic bags
☆ sticky tape
☆ any other interesting bits and pieces you have to hand.

> One of the first spells we witness Harry and his friends learning at Hogwarts is *Wingardium Leviosa*, the levitation spell, during their Charms lesson in *Philosopher's Stone*. Later, Harry, Ron and Hermione bond while using this spell to fight off the troll in the girls' bathroom.
>
> This activity sets students their own levitation challenge, but without the benefit of a magic wand!

## What to do

1. Organise the students into groups and give each one their bag or tray.

2. Explain the challenge: using the equipment given, they must find a way to "levitate" their feather over the greatest distance possible. Students may touch the feather only once, to set it on its way. Other items may touch the feather but, if they do, students may not touch the item that is touching the feather.

   There is no one particular way to solve this challenge – no specific "answer". Encourage your students to experiment and try out different ideas. Although there is an element of competition with this activity, stress that you will be awarding points for creativity, as well as for distance.

3. Give the students sufficient time to work on the challenge in their groups.

4. Each group demonstrates their feather levitating skills to the rest of the students. Agree on demonstration criteria beforehand. For example, each group may be permitted three attempts to demonstrate their method, or to demonstrate two alternative methods. In either case, the attempt that achieves the greatest distance may be taken as their response to the challenge.

# Literary lifeboat

## Focus areas
Literacy (speaking and listening), argument and reason

## Organisation
Students work as a whole group.

## Resources
A set of **Character cards** – make your own, with one card for each character described on page 37

> This well-known activity is given a Harry Potter twist, to enable students to develop their skills in reasoned argument.

## What to do

1. Explain the premise. Each student will be representing a character from the Harry Potter series. All the characters are on a sinking ship and the lifeboat doesn't have enough room for all of them. One of them must be left behind. But who?

2. Place the set of **Character cards** in a hat. Each student pulls out one card to determine which character they will represent. They must first complete a small character identification quiz, by using the description written on the card to guess the name of the character.

3. In turn, each student tells who they are and gives a brief summary of their role in the books. They then state their case for why their character should be allowed to remain safely in the lifeboat.

4. Once everyone has presented their case, there is a secret vote for who should remain behind. Students write the name of the character they would most like to leave behind on a slip of paper. The votes are counted.

5. The three characters with the highest number of votes take the hot seats. Once again, each one states their case, but the other students may now ask them questions or challenge their position as well.

6. Everyone votes for one of the three hot-seated characters. The character with the most votes is deemed to be ejected from the lifeboat.

**Note**: Encourage students to think deeply about the role of each character in the books and about their choice of who should be left behind. For example, they shouldn't just vote for Dudley Dursley because he is an unpleasant character and they don't like him. Think about his role in the book – not just from a reader's perspective but from a writer's perspective too. How would the story be different if Dudley wasn't in it?

Characters to use for your own set of Character cards

Create one card for each character described here. The student must guess the name on the card they draw, based on the description provided.

| | |
|---|---|
| A French beauty with seemingly magnetic attraction for many males | A student who is noted for her dedication to divination and kissing |
| A nosy journalist who likes to bend the truth | A lazy civil servant with a gambling problem |
| A dreamy student whose father is a newspaper man | A large, somewhat dim boy, much adored by his parents |
| An elf who was set free with a sock | A red-haired (though balding) civil servant |
| A hapless teacher who loses her job in a ministry shake-up | A centaur who is more prepared to talk with humans than most of his kind |
| An all-round successful student whose life ends tragically | A crusty member of the school staff, who has a cat as his offsider |
| A beautiful student whose friend betrays a resistance movement at the school | The somewhat unpredictable familiar of a very bright witch |
| An untrustworthy elf who transforms into an ally | A bathroom-haunting ghost |

# Hogwarts staff meeting (aka the Great Debate)

## Focus areas

Literacy (speaking and listening), argument and reason

## Organisation

Students work as a whole group, divided into two opposing teams.

## Resources

Your chosen debate topic from the **Great Debate topics** (page 39) (if choosing from these suggestions)

> In this activity, students will debate some controversial questions related to the Harry Potter series, drawing on their skills of reasoned argument as well as their actual knowledge of the series.

## What to do

1. Divide the students into two opposing teams and advise them of the point of view (affirmative or negative) they will be supporting. Provide the debate topic chosen from the **Great Debate topics**, or invite students to suggest their own topic to debate, and give the two teams some time to prepare their arguments.

2. Arrange the two teams facing each other and toss a coin to decide which team the first speaker will come from. Teams then take turns in presenting their arguments. Every student should participate and have a chance to speak in support of their team.

3. Give all students the chance to cross the floor. If they have been persuaded by the opposing team's arguments, they may express their opinion by voting with their feet.

4. At this point there may be a clear winner and the debate may end here. If the verdict still lies in the balance, however, open the floor for questions. Any student may ask a question of the opposing team but, if possible, questions and answers should proceed in an orderly manner, with the teams taking turns to ask one question.

5. Provide another opportunity to vote and cross the floor. Students are free to change their minds if they wish.

6. Conclude with a discussion of the issues raised and students' reasons for supporting the side they chose.

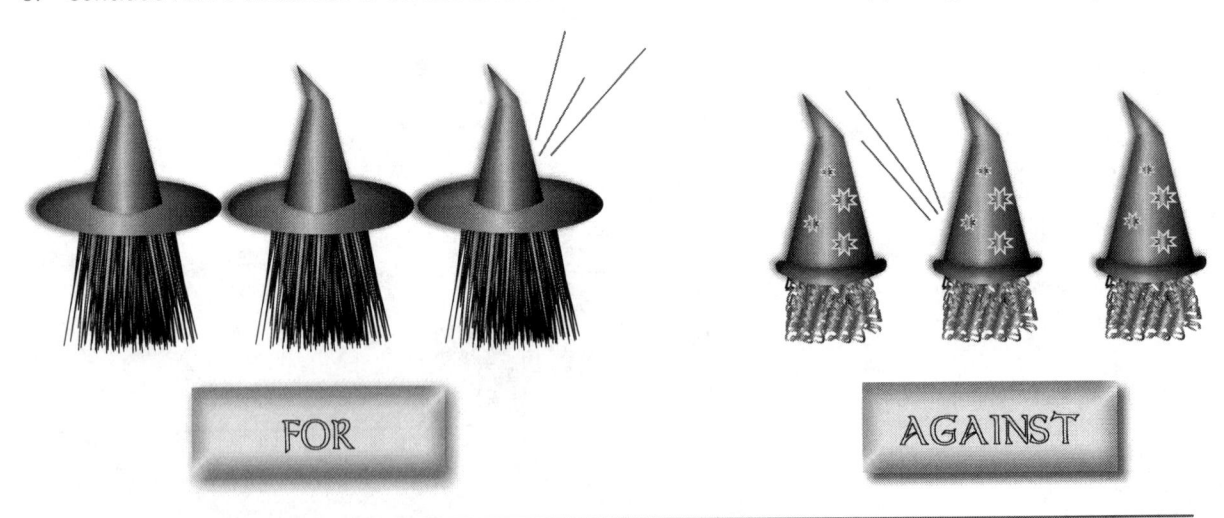

FOR

AGAINST

Great Debate topics

Choose one of these topics, or students may come up with their own.

## Should Slytherin be disbanded?

History shows us that Slytherin has produced more Dark wizards and witches than any other Hogwarts house. This record raises the question, should Slytherin house be disbanded? It is not proposed that Slytherin students be expelled from the school, but that the four houses become three and that the students from Slytherin be divided amongst the remaining houses equally.

**For:**　　Yes, Slytherin house should be disbanded.

**Against:**　　No, Slytherin house should remain a part of Hogwarts.

## Hermione's SPEW campaign was misguided

In *Harry Potter and the Goblet of Fire*, Hermione starts a campaign fighting for elf rights. She calls it SPEW – the Society for the Promotion of Elfish Welfare. She finds it very difficult to drum up support for her campaign and eventually takes to knitting hats and other garments and leaving them around Gryffindor Tower, in the hope that an unsuspecting house-elf will pick them up and be freed. Hermione believes ardently that the slavery-like conditions of the house-elves are wrong, but Ron insists that the elves like to live in this way.

**For:**　　Yes, Hermione's campaign was misguided. She should leave the house-elves alone.

**Against:**　　No, Hermione's campaign was not misguided. House-elves deserve better conditions, whether they want them or not.

## Snape was basically an evil man who did some good things

Even after his death and the end of the series, opinions are still divided over that enigmatic Professor of Potions, Severus Snape. We know that ultimately, like Harry, Snape was Dumbledore's man through and through. However, does that excuse him for making Harry's life a misery, not to mention Neville's, and for displaying incredible bias towards Slytherin?

**For:**　　Snape was basically a bad character who did some good things.

**Against:**　　No, Snape was basically a good character who did some bad things.

# Dynamic discussion

## Focus areas

Literacy (speaking and listening), critical thinking

## Organisation

Students work in large or small groups.

## Resources

Copy or copies of the **Discussion questions** (pages 42–43)
Paper, reusable sticky notes etc
Quaffle (eg, basketball or similar)
Reflective journals (optional)

> There is enough material in the Harry Potter series for several years' worth of discussions. Many of the themes in the books lend themselves to thoughtful discussion, leading into the exploration of philosophical issues. Dumbledore's speeches invariably provide plenty of food for thought as he imparts his considerable wisdom to Harry in each book, but there are also some more light-hearted questions to consider. Discussing literature in this way greatly enhances students' critical reading and thinking skills.

## What to do

Various approaches to this in-depth discussion activity are possible, as the suggestions below indicate. The following principles and processes are suggested whatever the particular approach you choose:

☆ The **Discussion questions** provide a starting point for discussion, but do encourage students to suggest their own questions for the group to discuss as well.

☆ Make it clear that your students are not expected to know the answer to these questions (most don't really have an "answer"), but they are expected to think about them. Encourage them, if they are called on to make a comment, to wonder, to speculate, to think aloud rather than say, "I don't know". Of course, it is assumed that you will have already developed an accepting climate in the classroom where students feel safe taking risks like this.

☆ Seat students in a circle or a horseshoe shape to allow for easy communication within the group.

☆ Encourage students to do most of the talking. Try to resist the temptation to tell them what you think, or to ask leading questions. Don't be afraid of silence.

## Some suggested approaches to discussion

### DISCUSSION DOODLE

This strategy is good for smaller groups of four or five students; if you have a larger group, you can split them up.

1. With the students around a table, with a large sheet of paper between them, read out the question.

2. As they discuss the question, students doodle. Encourage them to sketch images and symbols, as well as to write words or phrases. As the discussion progresses, the group will develop a giant doodle demonstrating their ideas, trains of thought and thinking processes.

3. If you have split up a larger group for this activity, each small group can share the doodles with the larger group.

## THINK, PAIR, NAME-STICK SHARE

1. Read the chosen question from the **Discussion questions** to the students (displaying it on an interactive whiteboard or handing out copies for students to refer to if you choose).

2. Give them about two minutes of individual thinking time. No one talks; each student just considers the question silently. If you like, they can jot down ideas during this time on sticky notes or individual white boards, or in reflective journals.

3. Students discuss the question with their discussion partner for a few minutes. (Arrange the pairings in advance.)

4. Call the students back to attention. Having previously written all the students' names on wooden craft sticks (or something similar) and stored them in a cup, you now pick out a student's name at random and ask them to start off the discussion. Put their name back in the cup after you read it. Continue calling on individual students using the name-sticks as the discussion develops. The goal of this strategy is to encourage maximum participation, rather than having just a few students dominate the discussion. Because all students have had a chance to both think about the question individually and discuss the question with their partner, it lessens the trepidation they may ordinarily feel if they are called on unexpectedly.

## TOSS THE QUAFFLE

1. Read the discussion question and allow a minute or two of thinking time.

2. Toss the quaffle (basketball or something similar) to one of the students.

3. This student gives an initial response to the question, before tossing the quaffle to another student to continue the discussion.

4. Continue in this way, for as long as the students have worthwhile comments to add to the discussion.

## REFLECTIVE JOURNAL

Whichever approach to group discussion you take, you may like to encourage students to keep a reflective journal in which to note down their thoughts and ideas after each discussion. Allow 10 minutes or so at the end of the session for students to write in their journal while the ideas are still fresh in their mind. This might also be an opportunity for students to think of questions of their own they would like to pursue.

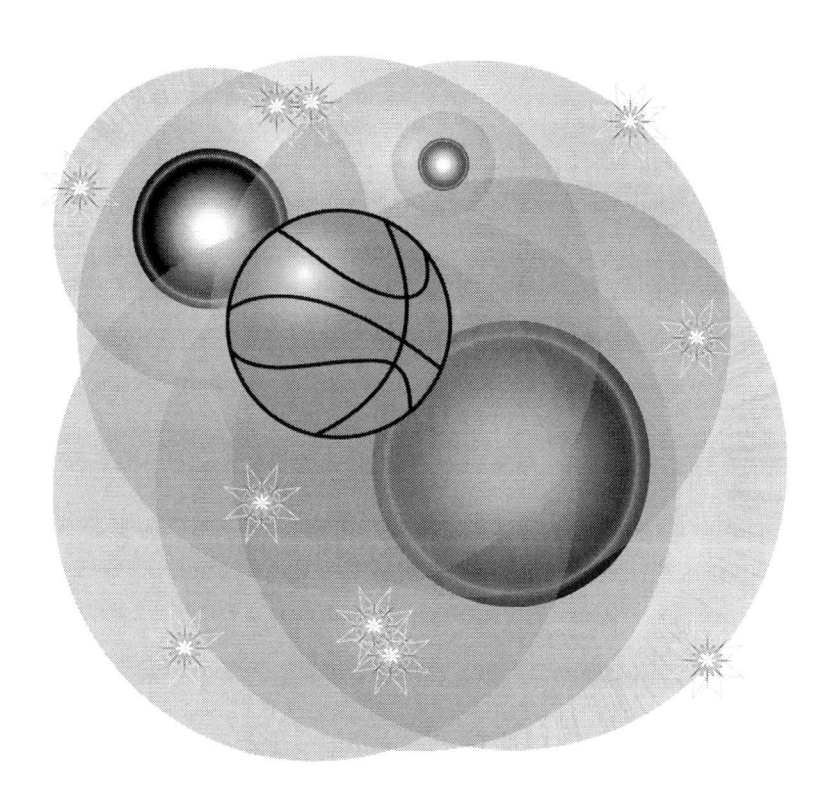

## Discussion questions

**1** "The truth is a beautiful and terrible thing, and should therefore be treated with great caution."

> Professor Dumbledore,
> *Harry Potter and the Philosopher's Stone*, Chapter 17

Discuss what Dumbledore means by this.

...................................................................

**2** "It is our choices Harry, that show what we truly are, far more than our abilities."

> Professor Dumbledore,
> *Harry Potter and the Chamber of Secrets*, Chapter 18

Do you agree with Dumbledore's statement?

...................................................................

**3** The prophecy in *Harry Potter and the Order of the Phoenix* could have applied to either Harry or Neville.

What if Voldemort had chosen Neville instead?

Could Neville have become the man Harry became?

Could he have defeated Voldemort?

...................................................................

**4** Are any characters in the series completely evil or completely good?

...................................................................

**5** Consider these two opposing quotes – one from the first book and one from the final book.

"There is no good or evil, there is only power, and those too weak to seek it."

> Professor Quirrell,
> *Harry Potter and the Philosopher's Stone*, Chapter 17

"...perhaps those who are best suited to power are those who have never sought it."

> Professor Dumbledore,
> *Harry Potter and the Deathly Hallows*, Chapter 35

Discuss.

...................................................................

**6** ... and in March several of the mandrakes threw a loud and raucous party in Greenhouse Three.

> *Harry Potter and the Chamber of Secrets*,
> Chapter 14

What would a mandrake do during a party?

...................................................................

**7** Who is the better friend to Harry – Ron or Hermione? Why?

What makes a good friend?

**8** "Of course it is happening inside your head, Harry, but why on earth should that mean it is not real?"

Professor Dumbledore,
*Harry Potter and the Deathly Hallows*, Chapter 35

Discuss.

**9** In the final book, Harry uses two Unforgivable Curses. In some circumstances, are normally unforgivable actions forgivable?

Is it forgivable to do unforgivable things for the greater good?

**10** Consider these lines from the Sorting Hat's song in Chapter 12 of *Harry Potter and the Goblet of Fire*, explaining how the four founders of Hogwarts' houses chose the members for their own house:

> … for each
> Did value different virtues
> In the ones they had to teach.
> By Gryffindor, the bravest were
> Prized far beyond the rest;
> For Ravenclaw, the cleverest
> Would always be the best;
> For Hufflepuff, hard workers were
> Most worthy of admission;
> And power-hungry Slytherin
> Loved those of great ambition.

Is ambition a virtue?

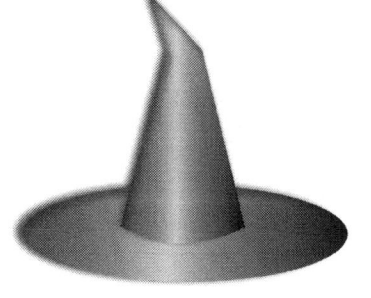

# Harry Potter and the learning ladders

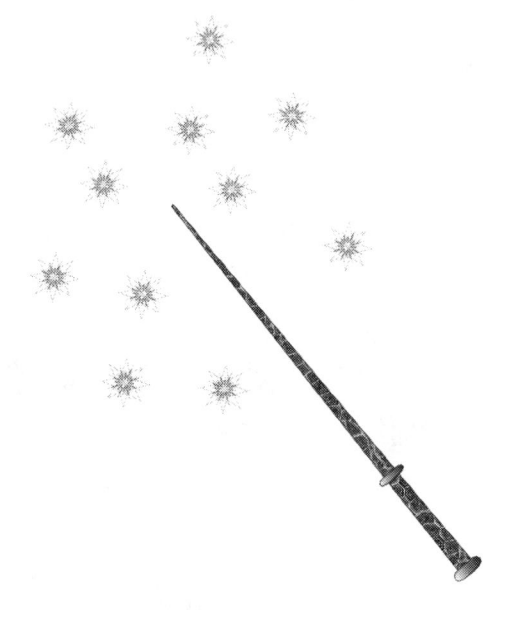

## Focus areas

Multiple

## Organisation

Students work individually or in pairs, or possibly as a whole group.

## Resources

Copies of the Learning ladder (pages 45–51) designed for the Harry Potter book you are focusing on

Other resources as required by the specific activity

> These learning ladders are designed to provide students with a range of thought-provoking activities to enhance their understanding and enjoyment of each book in the series. Loosely based on the ideas of both Bloom's taxonomy and Gardner's multiple intelligences, they are also influenced by the three-level ladder developed by Wilson and Murdoch (2008).

## What to do

There are really many different ways in which you can use these learning ladders. For example, you might use them:

☆ as an individual contract if you only have one Harry Potter reader in your class who needs some extension

☆ with groups of students who can work on the activities individually or in pairs, either in class time or as homework assignments

☆ as a whole group exercise, focusing on individual activities you have picked out to do in a more in-depth way.

As a guide, it is suggested that students complete at least three activities from each ladder, one from each row. However, as this approach is flexible as well, students may well choose to do more than three.

# Learning ladder: *Harry Potter and the Philosopher's Stone*

Starting at the bottom, choose at least one activity from each row. Your three answers will then show: (1) what you know or understand; (2) how you can analyse or organise information; and (3) how you can be creative.

| LEARNING FOCUS | WORD | MATHEMATICAL | VISUAL | MUSICAL | TACTILE |
|---|---|---|---|---|---|
| **CREATE** | Was Dumbledore being honest when he told Harry what he saw in the Mirror of Erised? What do you think he saw? What would you see? | Create a floor plan of one room in Hogwarts, eg, the Great Hall, Gryffindor common room, Harry's dormitory. Include a scale. | Choose a scene from the book to illustrate. Would it be a suitable choice for the front cover? Why or why not? | Record yourself reading an extract from the book. Add suitable sound effects and background music. | Create a board game using the events of the book as a guide. |
| **APPLY/ANALYSE** | Create a glossary explaining the meanings of all the new words we learn in this book. | Create 10 money problems using wizard currency – eg, how many knuts in 10 galleons? Include an answer sheet. | Draw a Venn diagram to compare and contrast two characters from the book, eg, Harry and Draco. | List five songs you would find on Harry's iPod and explain your choices. Choose another character and do the same. | Design a Muggle version of Quidditch that can be played on the ground. Explain the rules and include a diagram. |
| **KNOW/ UNDERSTAND** | Write the letters A–Z down the left-hand side of your page. Try to find at least one word related to this book for each letter of the alphabet. | How many students do you think there are at Hogwarts? Use evidence from the book to justify your answer. | List all the information you can learn about the book from the front and back covers (not including the blurb). | List all the information that we learn about Hogwarts from the Sorting Hat song and the school song. | Watch the film. How does it differ from the book? Why do you think it differs in these ways? |

© Essential Resources Educational Publishers Ltd, 2012

# Learning ladder: *Harry Potter and the Chamber of Secrets*

Starting at the bottom, choose at least one activity from each row. Your three answers will then show: (1) what you know or understand; (2) how you can analyse or organise information; and (3) how you can create.

| LEARNING FOCUS | WORD | MATHEMATICAL | VISUAL | MUSICAL | TACTILE |
|---|---|---|---|---|---|
| **CREATE** (3) | Write the first chapter of Gilderoy Lockhart's autobiography, *Magical Me*. | Draw a map of Diagon Alley and Knockturn Alley, showing the location of shops and other buildings we know of. | Create an alternative front cover that will give different information to that available from the cover(s) you have seen for this book. | Create a "mix CD" containing a collection of music that could be played at the Deathday Party. | Make a model of The Burrow using whatever materials you like. |
| **APPLY/ANALYSE** (2) | Imagine Lockhart sent himself a singing Valentine. What would it say? | Make a timeline of events from when Harry was born to the end of this book. | Compare and contrast two of the covers that have been used for this book. | List five songs that you think you would find on Gilderoy Lockhart's iPod. Explain your choices. | Keep a diary of your own for a week. |
| **KNOW/ UNDERSTAND** (1) | Collect as much information as possible on Gilderoy Lockhart. | Use information given in Chapter 8, "The Deathday Party", to work out the year in which the events in this book are taking place. | Collect at least three different images of cover art for this book. What information does each cover give? | Find a piece of music that you think could represent phoenix song. | Have a conversation with Tom Riddle's diary online at bit.ly/SJCOL |

© Essential Resources Educational Publishers Ltd, 2012

# Learning ladder: *Harry Potter and the Prisoner of Azkaban*

Starting at the bottom, choose at least one activity from each row. Your three answers will then show: (1) what you know or understand; (2) how you can analyse or organise information; and (3) how you can create.

| LEARNING FOCUS | WORD | MATHEMATICAL | VISUAL | MUSICAL | TACTILE |
|---|---|---|---|---|---|
| **3 CREATE** | What if Buckbeak had been found innocent? Create a new ending using a flow chart or a story map. | Using information from the first three books, create your own version of the Marauder's Map. | Create a visual way of showing the timeline of events in the time travel episode. | Create an original piece of music that could be used to signify the presence of Dementors. | Make an original advertisement for the Knight Bus, suitable for TV, radio or print. |
| **2 APPLY/ANALYSE** | Sirius was freed by Harry and Hermione on 6 June. Find out what happened on this date in 1944. Are there other examples of coinciding dates in this and other books? | Make a pie chart showing a typical day at Hogwarts for Harry. Do the same for Hermione. Compare the two charts. | Design a new Wanted poster for Sirius Black that reflects what we learn about him in this book. | Harry misses the Sorting in this book. Write a song that the Sorting Hat might have sung in this year. | Find some willing volunteers and attempt to read their tea leaves. |
| **1 KNOW/ UNDERSTAND** | List all the clues you can find that hint at Remus Lupin being a werewolf. | Make a series of maths problems based on the Knight Bus fares. Include an answer sheet. | Choose one of the characters we meet for the first time in this book and draw this character. | Listen to the soundtrack of the film version of this book. Which piece of music is your favourite? Why? | Research the art of telling the future through reading tea leaves. |

# Learning ladder: *Harry Potter and the Goblet of Fire*

Starting at the bottom, choose at least one activity from each row. Your three answers will then show: (1) what you know or understand; (2) how you can analyse or organise information; and (3) how you can create.

© Essential Resources Educational Publishers Ltd, 2012

| LEARNING FOCUS | WORD | MATHEMATICAL | VISUAL | MUSICAL | TACTILE |
|---|---|---|---|---|---|
| **3** CREATE | Imagine you are a student of Beauxbatons or Durmstrang. Write a letter home describing some of your time at Hogwarts. | Construct a table showing what might have been the results from the Quidditch World Cup qualifying rounds. Include the information given in the book. | Create a poster to advertise the Triwizard Tournament. | Write an extra wizard-type verse for either the Irish or the Bulgarian anthem. Do the same for the anthem of your own country or a country you would like to live in. | Design what could be a fourth task for the Triwizard Tournament and find a way to present your idea. |
| **2** APPLY/ANALYSE | Use a mind map or a flow chart to organise the most important elements of the plot of this book. | How much would Harry's 1000 Galleon prize money weigh if 1 Galleon is worth GBP 5 (convert to your own currency if it differs) and it has the same value as gold, gram for gram? Give answers for 9 ct, 18 ct and 24 ct gold. | Consider the colours associated with each house. Why do you think J.K. Rowling chose those colours in each case? | Choose five songs that the Weird Sisters might have played at the Yule Ball. | Create a maze and challenge some other students or your teacher to solve it. How long does it take them? |
| **1** KNOW/ UNDERSTAND | List all the information we learn about Beauxbatons and Durmstrang. What other questions do you still have about these schools? | How much would the Weasley twins have won if Bagman gave them odds of:<br>30–1<br>50–1<br>66–1<br>(Don't forget the funny wand.) | Find several examples of promotional posters for the *Goblet of Fire* film. Describe the elements they have in common. | Find the lyrics for the Irish and the Bulgarian national anthems. What do they have in common? | Identify a scene from the film that differs from how you imagined it when reading the book. Describe how you would have filmed it if you were the director. |

# Learning ladder: *Harry Potter and the Order of the Phoenix*

Starting at the bottom, choose at least one activity from each row. Your three answers will then show: (1) what you know or understand; (2) how you can analyse or organise information; and (3) how you can create.

| LEARNING FOCUS | WORD | MATHEMATICAL | VISUAL | MUSICAL | TACTILE |
|---|---|---|---|---|---|
| **CREATE** (3) | "Remember my last, Petunia." Write Dumbledore's last letter to Petunia Dursley. | Using your imagination, as well as information from the book, create a graph to show the circulation figures of *The Quibbler* for the year, and analyse the trends. | Create a t-shirt design that could be worn by **either** members of Dumbledore's Army **or** the Order of the Phoenix. | In a similar style to "Weasley Is Our King", write a song or chant for another member of the Gryffindor team and one for a Slytherin team member. | Construct a board game or similar based on the events that happen in the Department of Mysteries. |
| **APPLY/ANALYSE** (2) | Choose a moment in the story and write a diary entry for it as Dolores Umbridge. | On a map of the United Kingdom, devise a key and use your best guesses to show all the journeys Harry makes this year. | Design a poster with a suitable message for display at St Mungo's, eg, "A clean cauldron keeps potions from becoming poisons". | Could Sirius Black really have been Stubby Boardman, lead singer of The Hobgoblins? Present arguments for and against. | With a partner, enact the scene between McGonagall and Umbridge after Harry leaves his careers advice interview. |
| **KNOW/ UNDERSTAND** (1) | Using information given in Chapter 7 and later in the book, compile a brochure that provides a visitor's guide to the Ministry of Magic. | Take an online Harry Potter numbers quiz at www.sporcle. com/games/ freakthegeekout/ hpnums | Examine as many different covers as you can find for this book. Can you identify which scene inspired each one? | Read the Sorting Hat's new song. Rephrase the information given and present it in another format. | Re-create one of Dolores Umbridge's ornamental plates, using a paper plate and other materials of your choice. |

# Learning ladder: *Harry Potter and the Half-Blood Prince*

Starting at the bottom, choose at least one activity from each row. Your three answers will then show: (1) what you know or understand; (2) how you can analyse or organise information; and (3) how you can create.

| LEARNING FOCUS | WORD | MATHEMATICAL | VISUAL | MUSICAL | TACTILE |
|---|---|---|---|---|---|
| **3 CREATE** | Write the back cover blurb for *Blood Brothers: My Life Amongst the Vampires* by Eldred Worple. | Investigate the use of the number 12 in Harry Potter's world. Do the same for prime numbers. Do you notice any patterns? | Design a new cover for Harry's battered copy of Advanced Potion Making. | Write the rest of the lyrics to Celestina Warbeck's "A Cauldron Full of Hot, Strong Love" (Chapter 16) and set it to music. | Create for your own family a version of Mrs Weasley's clock, which tells her when the family are "in mortal peril". |
| **2 APPLY/ANALYSE** | "Dumbledore says people find it far easier to forgive others for being wrong than being right" (Chapter 5). Discuss this statement. | Draw a floor plan of Weasley's Wizard Wheezes, using a scale, a key and as much information from the book as possible. | Choose one of the products sold in Weasley's Wizard Wheezes. Design an advertisement for it to publish in the Daily Prophet. | Choose a song that might have been played at Dumbledore's funeral. Explain your choice. | Make a scrapbook containing images, artefacts and/or words to recount the main events of the book. |
| **1 KNOW/ UNDERSTAND** | Retell the main events of the book using 150 words or fewer. | Make a timeline of the memories Dumbledore shows Harry in the pensieve. | Create a visual flow chart of the various student pairings and relationships this year. | Harry misses the Sorting Hat's song again but asks what it said. Write a verse or two that the Hat might have sung at the feast. | Identify and describe the main differences between the book and the film. What is the impact of these changes? |

# Learning ladder: *Harry Potter and the Deathly Hallows*

Starting at the bottom, choose at least one activity from each row. Your three answers will then show: (1) what you know or understand; (2) how you can analyse or organise information; and (3) how you can create.

| LEARNING FOCUS | WORD | MATHEMATICAL | VISUAL | MUSICAL | TACTILE |
|---|---|---|---|---|---|
| **CREATE** | Write an extra chapter that tells the story of the attempted theft of Gryffindor's sword by Neville, Ginny and Luna. | Scrimgeour thought Dumbledore had left a coded message for Hermione. Devise a code and use it to write such a message. | Design a set of commemorative coins, including a galleon, sickle and a knut, celebrating the events of the book. Include both sides of each coin. | Write and record a programme for Potterwatch, including theme music or jingle. | Imagine a time when sales of Deathly Hallows are slipping. Design and make a free gift to be given away with the book. |
| **APPLY/ANALYSE** | What parallels can be drawn between the events of the Deathly Hallows and the Second World War? | Rate each chapter on criteria of your choice, eg, suspense and excitement. Plot the results on a graph. | Compare the Bloomsbury and Scholastic covers of the book. Why do you think they chose such different scenes? Which do you prefer? Why? | Choose five characters and give them Potterwatch nicknames. Explain your choices. | Design and make a chocolate frog card for two of the following characters: Dobby; Severus Snape; Gellert Grindelwald. |
| **KNOW/ UNDERSTAND** | Starting with Hedwig, we lose a lot of characters in this book. Write an obituary column that includes all the characters who don't survive. | Using a ruler and compass, draw the Deathly Hallows symbol in a range of sizes. Develop a formula to calculate the area of each space within the symbol. | Make an illustrated children's book telling the "Tale of the Three Brothers". | Modify an existing song to retell the events of one or more chapters in the book. | Do you agree with the film-maker's choice of where to split the book in order to make the two *Deathly Hallows* films? Why or why not? Where would you have chosen to split it? Explain. |

# References and further resources

Anelli, M (2008) *Harry, A History: The true story of a boy wizard, his fans, and life inside the Harry Potter phenomenon*. New York: Pocket Books.

Baggett, D & Klein, S E (Eds) (2004) *Harry Potter and Philosophy: If Aristotle ran Hogwarts*. Chicago: Open Court.

Gibbs, N (2007) J.K. Rowling. *TIME* magazine, 19 December 2007, accessed online at: http://www.time.com/time/specials/2007/personoftheyear/0,28757,1690753,00.html #ixzz1KdDW1Wf3

Gross, M U M, Macleod, B, Drummond, D & Merrick, C (2003) *Gifted Students in Primary Schools: Differentiating the curriculum*. Sydney: Gifted Education Research, Resource and Information Centre.

Halstead, J W (2009) *Some of My Best Friends Are Books: Guiding gifted readers from preschool to high school*, 3rd edn. Scottsdale, AZ: Great Potential Press.

Mathew, K L & Adams, D C (2009) I love your book, but I love my version more: Fanfiction in the English language arts classroom. *The ALAN Review*, 36(3): 35–41.

Rowling, J.K. (1997) *Harry Potter and the Philosopher's Stone*. London: Bloomsbury.

Rowling, J.K. (1998) *Harry Potter and the Chamber of Secrets*. London: Bloomsbury.

Rowling, J.K. (1999) *Harry Potter and the Prisoner of Azkaban*. London: Bloomsbury.

Rowling, J.K. (2000) *Harry Potter and the Goblet of Fire*. London: Bloomsbury.

Rowling, J.K. (2001) *Fantastic Beasts and Where to Find Them*. London: Bloomsbury.

Rowling, J.K. (2003) *Harry Potter and the Order of the Phoenix*. London: Bloomsbury.

Rowling, J.K. (2005) *Harry Potter and the Half-Blood Prince*. London: Bloomsbury.

Rowling, J.K. (2007) *Harry Potter and the Deathly Hallows*. London. Bloomsbury.

Vogler, Christopher (1992) *The Writer's Journey: Mythic structure for storytellers and screenwriters*. Studio City, CA: Michael Wiese Productions.

Wilson, J & Murdoch, K (2008) *Learning for Themselves*. Victoria, Australia: Curriculum Corporation.

## Recommended websites

| | |
|---|---|
| The Harry Potter Alliance thehpalliance.org | This army of fans, activists, nerdfighters, teenagers, wizards and Muggles is dedicated to fighting for social justice with the greatest weapon we have – love. |
| The Harry Potter Lexicon www.hp-lexicon.info | Information and minute details from the series arranged in an encyclopaedic fashion. A great resource. |
| J.K. Rowling Official Site www.jkrowling.com | Includes a biography, frequently asked questions and extra stuff. There are also hidden surprises available on the site for diligent fans who solve various puzzles. |
| The Leaky Cauldron the-leaky-cauldron.org | Lots of news and features, including its own version of *The Quibbler*, regular competitions and the largest Harry Potter social network on the internet. |
| MuggleNet www.mugglenet.com | Features news, views, forums, discussions and sections for fanfiction and fanart. |
| Pottermore www.pottermore.com | J.K. Rowling's newest venture. An online interactive experience built from the reading of the Harry Potter series. |

CPSIA information can be obtained at www.ICGtesting.com
Printed in the USA
BVOC01s0958080616

451209BV00014B/150/P

9 781927 143124